BILLY SUNDAY
AND OTHER POEMS

CARL
SANDBURG

A Harvest Original
Harcourt Brace & Company
San Diego   New York   London

BILLY SUNDAY AND OTHER POEMS

EDITED AND WITH AN INTRODUCTION
BY GEORGE HENDRICK
AND WILLENE HENDRICK

Copyright © 1993 by Maurice C. Greenbaum and Frank M.
Parker as Trustees of the Carl Sandburg Family Trust
Compilation, Introduction, and Notes copyright © 1993 by
George Hendrick and Willene Hendrick

Acknowledgments and permissions appear on page 116,
which constitutes a combination of the copyright page.

Library of Congress Cataloging-in-Publication Data
Sandburg, Carl, 1878–1967.
Billy Sunday and other poems/by Carl Sandburg; edited with
an introduction by George Hendrick and Willene Hendrick.
—1st ed.
p.   cm.
"A Harvest original."
ISBN 0-15-162130-6
ISBN 0-15-662144-4 (pbk.)
1. Sunday, Billy, 1862–1935—Poetry.   I. Hendrick, George.
II. Hendrick, Willene, 1928–   .   III. Title.
PS3537.A618B5   1993
811'.52—dc20   93-4863

Designed by Lori J. McThomas

Printed in the United States of America

First Edition

A B C D E

To Margaret, Janet, and Helga Sandburg

TABLE OF CONTENTS

ix

Introduction

When Carl Sandburg, the Pulitzer Prize–winning poet and Lincoln biographer, died in 1967 he left hundreds of unpublished poems. His daughter Margaret edited a volume of them, which she called *Breathing Tokens,* in 1978, but still more of his strong poems remained. From his files now housed in the University of Illinois at Urbana-Champaign library here is Sandburg once again: fighting a religious fraud; arguing for economic, racial, and social justice; writing profiles and love poems and anti-war poems; daydreaming; and still speaking directly and forcefully to readers.

These unpublished or uncollected or unexpurgated poems are arranged in twelve sections. This introduction provides a brief literary, historical, or social context for a better understanding and appreciation of the poems in each of the twelve sections of the book.

Sandburg regarded the evangelist Billy Sunday as a dangerous demagogue, a subversive influence on American life and democracy itself. The first section in this volume contains two of Sandburg's most forceful poems about the man he called a "crowd trickster."

The poem "Billy Sunday" played a major role in the publication history of *Chicago Poems.* After a long apprenticeship as a poet, in January 1916 the newspaper reporter Sandburg sent the manuscript of his *Chicago Poems* to Alfred Harcourt, then a young editor at the Henry Holt firm. From his first reading, Harcourt wanted to publish the manuscript, but he encountered problems in getting the text past the more senior members of that publishing company, for, as he wrote Sandburg, "its subject matter and strength seemed to them rather raw for their imprint." Harcourt actually removed the poem about Billy Sunday and a few others from the text: "For obvious reasons," he wrote the poet, "we think the poems, the subjects of which are living people referred to by name, should certainly be omitted." Sandburg set to work and made the necessary changes to ensure that the manuscript was acceptable to the publisher.

The Billy Sunday poem was retitled "To a Contemporary Bunk-shooter," the evangelist Sunday was no longer referred to by name, and language thought to be offensive was omitted. Sandburg wrote Harcourt on February 4, 1916, that his revisions should make it acceptable "to all but the most hidebound and creed-drilled religionists." With his strong feelings on the subject of false religious prophets, Sandburg further condemned Sunday: "He is the most conspicuous single embodiment in this country of the crowd leader or crowd operative who uses jungle methods, stark voodoo stage effects, to play hell with democracy." It is not surprising, therefore, that Sandburg's original poem "Billy Sunday" is more powerful and evocative than the revised "To a Contemporary Bunkshooter." It deserves its place as the title poem in this volume.

The "Billy Sunday" poem had appeared in two radical magazines—*The Masses* and the *International Socialist Review*—before Sandburg was required to make changes for Henry Holt. Sandburg wrote one other poem about Billy Sunday, "God's Children," but it never appeared, perhaps because earlier editors found it too blasphemous for their readers.

The second section is entirely devoted to Sandburg's poetic meditation on the sinking of the steamship the *Eastland*. Loaded with about 2,500 workers and their families who were being "treated" to a company picnic by their employer, the ship sank in the Chicago River on July 24, 1915, drowning more than eight hundred people. Sandburg wrote an angry prose piece for the September 1915 issue of the *International Socialist Review*, charging that William C. Redfield, Secretary of Commerce, had been derelict in his duties: "Why didn't Redfield co-ordinate the human units, the high salaried bureau heads under him, so as to stop a cranky, unstable ancient hoodoo tub like the *Eastland* from going loaded with 2,500 lives? There's one answer. Business required it." He said that the workers on board the *Eastland*, headed for the picnic in Michigan, had been forced to purchase tickets for the excursion and that they were to wear white shoes and purchase white hats, so that a photograph of the thousands of workers would show up well in advertising copy for the company. In Sandburg's estimation, "Grim industrial feudalism stands with dripping and red hands behind the whole *Eastland* affair."

"The *Eastland*" contains some of Sandburg's most powerful images of the human misery he saw daily in the lives of working people in the industrialized Chicago he knew so well. Obviously too "raw," too radical for publication when it was written, "The *Eastland*" appears here for the first time. In this poem Sandburg was quite clearly, as *The Western Comrade* called him, "the rising poet of the revolution."

Three of Sandburg's powerful anti-war poems comprise the third section of this volume. Before the United States was drawn into World War I, Sandburg wrote many poems opposing the war. Early on in his life, he had been a Socialist organizer, and at first, he opposed the war, but his radicalism became tempered. Once it was clear that the United States was going to enter the war, Sandburg supported Wilson and the pro-war forces, as many Socialists did not. Sandburg's changing views about this particular war may have influenced his decision not to publish or collect these anti-war poems.

"Planked Whitefish" is one of the strongest of Sandburg's early war poems. The reference to genital mutilation was, of course, unacceptable to publishers at that time, and the descriptions of the horrors of war were too vivid for most readers.

"Ashes and Dreams" appeared in the May 1915 issue of the *International Socialist Review* but was never collected. Without being maudlin, it was, as Penelope Niven observes in her biography of Sandburg, "an ode to the mothers of the world whose sons and dreams were lost to war."

"Vaudeville: 1916," appearing here for the first time, sharply contrasts scenes of Chicago vaudeville with those of the terrible battles in Europe: the perfect bodies of the women trapeze artists with the maimed and starving people overseas, the clown's mock danger against the horrors of the battle of Verdun. Sandburg's poetic intent is clear and telling as the German crown prince and the French general "ask how the weather looks for new troop movements." Sandburg omits the grisly casualty figures for that battle, but the vivid images of entertainment and death are bound together unforgettably in this poem.

Sandburg the imagist poet is featured in the fourth section. In his most famous poem, "Fog," the image is memorable, the scene universal, but there is no context for it. In the poems included here, Sandburg, the poet with a social conscience, the walker in the city of Chicago, the observer of industrial life, the reader of history, turned from "pure" images to images in social and historical context.

"Painted Fishes" moves the imagist poem into the saloon, mingling heavy beer glasses with the delicacy of the green-painted fishes on the red-laquered tray. The reader, drawn into the scene, can see the beer foam covering the fishes, can hear the steins slide on the tray, eroding their fins. No stranger to saloons, Sandburg creates a beautiful picture out of the sawdust-floored, raucous world of bars.

Amy Lowell and several other imagist poets, including Sandburg, were influenced by Chinese poetry and paintings. When Sandburg visited Amy Lowell in Massachusetts, he met the translator Florence Ayscough. Enthusiastic about her Chinese translations, he turned some of them into free verse, and in "These Valleys Seem Old," he combined imagism and social criticism. Sandburg wrote Amy Lowell about permission to print his poems suggested by the Ayscough translations, and in September 1919 Lowell responded that Ayscough would not give the necessary permission because she did not find the renderings at all exact, although she thought they were very beautiful. The four poems in "These Valleys Seem Old," inexact renditions though they may be, are as beautiful as the scenes on the scroll paintings. Because of Ayscough's objections, these poems remained unpublished until now.

Sandburg was a reader of history as well as a writer about up-to-the-minute Chicago news. He gave serious thought to Napoleon, bloody battles, and tyrants who disappear in the mists of time. The images in "Napoleon" and Sandburg's other imagist poetry linger in the mind, some as stealthy as heavy fog, some as bright as the painted fishes, some as continually echoing as the "sluffing" sound of the workingmen's feet on the sidewalk.

An acute observer of people around him, Sandburg often wrote poetic portraits; four of these make up the fifth grouping of poems in this collection. One of his most vivid poems was about Chicago's Mrs. Potter Palmer, ruler of that city's social life. Mrs. Palmer was "exclusive," Sandburg declared, and he viewed exclusivity as the ultimate social insult. Years later he told his friend Gregory d'Alessio that the word he hated most in the English language was "EX-CLO-O-O-O-SIVE!"

Sandburg had been thinking of his portrait of Mrs. Potter Palmer for over a decade before he wrote about her in "Magical Confusion." Reuben W. Borough, a reporter for the Chicago *Daily Socialist* when he met Sandburg in 1907, provided a memorable portrait of Sandburg's hates and loves in his "The Sandburg I Remember":

We were both country boys, lonely at night in the cold hall rooms of cold rooming houses, drawn and held together by common ideals, passions, prejudices. I was delighted to find that he was as militant an equalitarian as I. . . . We were both out gunning for Mrs. Potter Palmer! Out of stubborn commitment to the common people and proud identification with the poor and disinherited, we were both at war with the capitalist system. And in addition to all this was our devotion to the vague, sometimes mystical, and always beautiful realm of poetry.

In contrast to Sandburg's derogatory treatment of the exclusive Mrs. Potter Palmer, he wrote sympathetic poetic portraits of the poor and disinherited. In "Pearl Diver" he wrote of the dishwasher in the kitchen who could overhear the gaiety in the restaurant but clearly could not join in the revelry. In "Jerry" Sandburg, the journalist poet with feminist sympathies, wrote about the abused woman who killed her brutish husband. Confined to prison for the rest of her life, she proclaimed, "I would do it again."

In "Taking on Suds Men Talk" Sandburg tells the story of a prostitute, and the way the poem is told is of particular interest. The narrator, Tom, tells the woman's story to I, the listener, probably Sandburg. Since Tom is reconstructing and condensing her story, he may not be representing the entire truth of her situation. The method of narration makes the woman's life even more tragic. As is usual, Sandburg is sympathetic to the downtrodden of the world.

Harry Golden observed in his impressionistic biography of the poet, "The problem of racial equality has never been far from Sandburg's mind." The four poems in this sixth section all deal with African Americans, racial relations, and racial equality. "Elizabeth Umpstead" was one of Sandburg's most dramatic poems on this theme. He never collected the poem, but it was used in Norman Corwin's successful play *The World of Carl Sandburg*, a production that toured the country and also played in New York. This poem was so powerful that wherever the actress Bette Davis recited it she was given a standing ovation. As Edgar Lee Masters's characters did in the Spoon River poems, Elizabeth Umpstead speaks from the grave and tells the truth of the ways she had been used by men.

In "Black Prophetess" the speaker is a simple black woman who stands on the street and warns of God's wrath and the coming destruction of the earth. She is absolutely convinced of her prophetic abilities, and the reporter presents her monologue without judgment or condescension.

In "Cleo" Sandburg describes with sympathy and understanding the simple country woman who had survived the terrible conditions endured by rural blacks after the Civil War and yet had remained at peace with her environment and her God.

Over 1,100 men and women (almost all black) were lynched in the United States from 1900 until the outbreak of World War I. As John Hope Franklin and Alfred A. Moss, Jr., noted in *From Slavery to Freedom: A History of Negro Americans*, "The South was far ahead of the rest of the country, but several Northern states, notably those in the Midwest, adhered to this ancient barbaric ritual of total disregard for the law." Sandburg was aware of lynchings in the Midwest. He had written about the blacks in Chicago, and he wrote a series of articles on the 1919 race riots in which thirty-eight people died. Published as *Chicago Race Riots: July 1919*, the work was praised by a contemporary critic as a "serious and intelligent investigation into conditions which made the race riots possible."

Sandburg submitted his poem about a lynching, called "Man, the Man-Hunter," to Louis Untermeyer for inclusion in *An American Miscellany*. Untermeyer was afraid that the language would arouse church groups and the Society for Suppression of Vice and requested revisions. Sandburg agreed to make changes, and he wrote to Untermeyer in March 1920:

> You're right about the S.O.B. Let it read, "crying 'Kill him, kill him, the . . . ,' " deleting "the Judean equivalent" and "Son of a Bitch." I would never have put this in but that it's come over me clear the last two or three years that in a group killing of a man, in a mobbing, the event reaches a point where all rationale is gone; such a term as "anarchist" and "traitor" or "Boche" or "Englander Schwein" disappears and they babble hysterically only one or two epithets, in our language usually a tenor of "Son of a Bitch" with a bass of "Cocksucker." Since some of the finest blood of the human family goes this way poets and painters have a right to try to employ it or at least not kid themselves about what actually happened at Golgotha. Since I've talked with men who were in the trenches and since I've seen race riots I am suspicious that the sponge of vinegar on the spear is a faked legend and what probably happened, if the historicity of Jesus is ever established, is that they cut off his genital organ and stuck it in his mouth. . . .

The poem "Planked Whitefish," included in the section of antiwar poems, also makes use of war/genital images. Sandburg's original version of the poem "Man, the Man-Hunter" is published in this collection.

The seventh section contains five poems drawn from Sandburg's experiences as a Chicago newspaper reporter. For twenty years, beginning in 1912, Sandburg worked first on the *Evening World,* then on the advertising-free *Day Book,* and finally on the *Daily News,* writing labor articles, reports on local events, and movie reviews.

During his days as a newspaper reporter, Sandburg recorded in poetry his impressions of Chicago life and events. He regarded these poems as his daily diary. In "Dailies," Sandburg the poet of the people, identified with the daily newspaper, "dirty and always fighting." In "Monday, One P.M." he wrote an experimental poem contrasting the visit of a reporter to I.W.W. headquarters, an overheard telephone conversation about a bulldog bitch, and a phone call to Amy Lowell, the high priestess of imagism. His hope, he said, was for the new poetry he was writing "to get at the real stuff of American life."

For a newspaper article about the movement of dinosaur bones and Egyptian tombs to the new Field Museum, Sandburg incorporated a Whitmanesque poem, "Big Stones of the Egyptian Tombs," by the "inspired reporter." In "The Rewrite Man Is Tired," he returns to the banality and sordidness of Chicago life, as reflected in the daily newspapers.

Sandburg often included spontaneous poems in his letters. He wrote Louis Untermeyer on September 26, 1919: "We have moved from Maywood to Elmhurst, a bigger place for the kids to grow up in, and more of a chance to raise the little ones ourselves instead of having the neighbor kid gangs take all their day and night. Also we are in debt now." The poem, "A Reporter in Debt," was then inserted as an integral part of the letter. It is both playful and somber as it presents the radical poet borrowing money to buy a house, for how could he write about the downtrodden unless he himself was being crushed by the system?

The eighth section contains four Sandburg poems about Edgar Lee Masters. Masters and Sandburg met in 1914, and they immediately became friends. Masters praised the "beautiful imagery" in Sandburg's poems, but also noted, "Most of them were shocking, forthright with a sudden turn of rude realism." A prominent Chicago attorney, Masters began to write poems about the Spoon River folk of his youth. His characters spoke from the grave about their lives, loves, disappointments, griefs, thwarted desires. Fearing his law practice would suffer if his identity were known, he at first published these poems under the pseudonym "Webster Ford."

Sandburg knew about Masters's secret poetic life and in "To Webster Ford" writes about the deeply divided man living the public life of a leading attorney and the secret life of a poet writing psychological tales of the people of Spoon River. Sandburg was generally on friendly terms with his fellow poets, but several incidents soured the Masters-Sandburg friendship. Masters thought Sandburg's class consciousness played a part in their growing coolness. One day Masters, who had been ill, met Sandburg on Michigan Avenue in Chicago. According to Masters, Sandburg "stopped with jealous fury in his eyes. He had read about the London wedding of my niece, and what right had a man born to the manner of Illinois to have a niece married to an English lieutenant under all those fashionable circumstances, with myself announced as the uncle who would have given away the bride except for his illness?" Sandburg's opinion, as he wrote his friend Alice Corbin Henderson, was that "Masters is getting a sicker man all the time" and that the problem was "psychic." Sandburg's "Edgar Lee Masters" and the poem that follows it express his growing disenchantment with the tormented man who could not reconcile the two worlds he created for himself.

Some years later Masters wrote what critics have called a "demonized" book on Lincoln, perhaps in response to Sandburg's sympathetic *Abraham Lincoln: The Prairie Years*. Sandburg's private poem about Masters's attack on Lincoln titled "On Rereading Edgar Lee Masters' Lincoln-the-Man Three Years after the First Reading" is one of his harshest utterances against a fellow poet.

During his long life, Sandburg wrote many love poems. A selection of these, previously unpublished, appears in the ninth section. Context in time and place and circumstance for these poems is not known. Titles taken from the poems themselves have been provided.

Sandburg's early love poems were rather Victorian in both form and content; in 1906 he published a romantic poem about an idealized woman which he called "Dream Girl." Two years later he met Lilian Steichen, whom he was to marry, and he sent that poem to her. The intellectual Steichen, a Socialist and a realist, responded that the dream girl is "not of our world to-day but of the Millennial Epoch of Rest. In our Epoch of Struggle girls must be made of sterner stuff." Lilian Steichen Sandburg was to have a profound influence on her husband's poetry. Sandburg in his later love poems abandoned Victorian idealism. The poems published here are passionate, realistic, and imagistic.

Perhaps as part of an unfinished portrait series, Sandburg wrote many poems about literary and historical figures. The tenth section of this volume contains a selection of these sketches. As a Chicago reporter, Sandburg interviewed writers who came to that city, and he met even more writers and artists when he was on his extended lecture and reading tours across the country. A reader of history and of major literary texts of the past, he was fascinated by such figures as Daniel Webster and Nathaniel Hawthorne. Sandburg was a man of many friendships, as his tribute to Eugene V. Debs demonstrates. Taken together, these portraits show Sandburg as sensitive literary critic and astute observer of writers and public figures.

Sandburg never published his intensely felt "Legal Midnight Hour," obviously written immediately after the execution of Sacco and Vanzetti in 1927. The poem appears here in the eleventh section.

Sacco and Vanzetti, two Italian-born anarchists living in Massachusetts, were arrested in 1920 and charged with the murder of two men in a payroll holdup. They were tried, convicted, and after seven years, executed. It was widely believed that they were innocent, that they were convicted because of their anarchistic beliefs, that they were found guilty in a kangaroo court, and that the evidence against them was tainted or faked. The Chicago *Daily*

News, where Sandburg worked throughout the 1920s, devoted thousands of column inches to this celebrated case, which mesmerized people all over the world. In his emotional, detail-filled poem, Sandburg indicated by that series of question marks after the last line that the controversy surrounding Sacco and Vanzetti would not die with their execution, as indeed it has not.

Popular magazines after the turn of this century carried many articles and stories, accompanied by dramatic line drawings, about men being executed by Mexican revolutionaries or French Foreign Legion firing squads. The twelfth and concluding section in this volume contains an untitled poem, here called "I Should Like to Be Hanged on a Summer Afternoon," in which Sandburg daydreams on this theme. Sandburg, the poet with a social conscience, envisions himself being executed in a carnival atmosphere. He faces his impending death bravely, but he does not explain any of the reasons why he is being put to death. It is clear, however, that he meets his fate refusing to recant whatever opinions or poems were unacceptable to the spectators.

Sandburg was a poet who wrote in the language of the people and for the people, who believed in social, economic, and racial justice, and who wanted to write poems understandable to the common man. As he once said, his poetry was to "sing, blab, chortel, yodel." Here from the dusty files of journals and from his kit bag of unpublished work are some of his best poems.

GEORGE HENDRICK
WILLENE HENDRICK

THE

EVANGELIST

BILLY SUNDAY

BILLY SUNDAY

You come along—tearing your shirt—yelling about Jesus.
  I want to know what the hell you know about Jesus?

Jesus had a way of talking soft, and everybody except a few
  bankers and higher-ups among the con men of Jerusalem
  liked to have this Jesus around because he never made any
  fake passes, and everything he said went and he helped the
  sick and gave the people hope.

You come along squirting words at us, shaking your fist and
  calling us all dam fools—so fierce the froth of your own spit
  slobbers over your lips—always blabbering we're all going to
  hell straight off and you know all about it.

I've read Jesus' words. I know what he said. You don't throw
  any scare into me. I've got your number. I know how much
  you know about Jesus.

He never came near clean people or dirty people but they felt
  cleaner because he came along. It was your crowd of bankers
  and business men and lawyers that hired the sluggers and
  murderers who put Jesus out of the running.

3

I say it was the same bunch that's backing you that nailed the
    nails into the hands of this Jesus of Nazareth. He had lined
    up against him the same crooks and strong-arm men now
    lined up with you paying your way.

This Jesus guy was good to look at, smelled good, listened
    good. He threw out something fresh and beautiful from the
    skin of his body and the touch of his hands wherever he
    passed along.

You, Billy Sunday, put a smut on every human blossom that
    comes in reach of your rotten breath belching about hell-fire
    and hiccuping about this man who lived a clean life in
    Galilee.

When are you going to quit making the carpenters build
    emergency hospitals for women and girls driven crazy with
    wrecked nerves from your goddam gibberish about Jesus? I
    put it to you again: What the hell do you know about Jesus?

Go ahead and bust all the chairs you want to. Smash a wagon
    load of furniture at every performance. Turn sixty
    somersaults and stand on your nutty head. If it wasn't for
    the way you scare the women and kids, I'd feel sorry for
    you and pass the hat.

I like to watch a good four-flusher work, but not when he
   starts people puking and calling for the doctor.

I like a man that's got guts and can pull off a great, original
   performance; but you—hell, you're only a bughouse peddler
   of second-hand gospel—you're only shoving out a phoney
   imitation of the goods this Jesus guy told us ought to be free
   as air and sunlight.

Sometimes I wonder what sort of pups born from mongrel
   bitches there are in the world less heroic, less typic of
   historic greatness than you.

You tell people living in shanties Jesus is going to fix it up all
   right with them by giving them mansions in the skies after
   they're dead and the worms have eaten 'em.

You tell $6 a week department store girls all they need is Jesus;
   you take a steel trust wop, dead without having lived, gray
   and shrunken at forty years of age, and you tell him to look
   at Jesus on the cross and he'll be all right.

You tell poor people they don't need any more money on pay
   day, and even if it's fierce to be out of a job, Jesus'll fix that
   all right, all right—all they gotta do is take Jesus the way
   you say.

I'm telling you this Jesus guy wouldn't stand for the stuff you're handing out. Jesus played it different. The bankers and corporation lawyers of Jerusalem got their sluggers and murderers to go after Jesus just because Jesus wouldn't play their game. He didn't sit in with the big thieves.

I don't want a lot of gab from a bunkshooter in my religion.

I won't take my religion from a man who never works except with his mouth and never cherishes a memory except the face of the woman on the American silver dollar.

I ask you to come through and show me where you're pouring out the blood of your life.

I've been out to this suburb of Jerusalem they call Golgotha, where they nailed Him, and I know if the story is straight it was real blood ran from his hands and the nail-holes, and it was real blood spurted out where the spear of the Roman soldier rammed in between the ribs of this Jesus of Nazareth.

GOD'S CHILDREN

    I hear Billy Sunday
    And the Kaiser and the Czar
    Talking about God
Like God was some pal of theirs,
Like the rest of us was in the cold outside,
Like they had been drinking beer with God,
Like as though they know whether God
Calls for a short beer or a gin fizz
Or whether God sleeps in a Y.M.C.A. dormitory
And never goes near a booze bazaar.

When I listen to Billy Sunday
Holler out loud
How God "hates a quitter,"
How God "hates a mutt,"
I can't help it—I feel just like God was some cheap dirty thing
    born from a fiddler's bitch and kicked from one back door
    to another.

THE

SINKING OF

THE *EASTLAND*

THE *EASTLAND*

Let's be honest now
For a couple of minutes
Even though we're in Chicago.

Since you ask me about it,
I let you have it straight;
My guts ain't ticklish about the *Eastland*.

It was a hell of a job, of course
To dump 2,500 people in their clean picnic clothes
All ready for a whole lot of real fun
Down into the dirty Chicago river without any warning.

Women and kids, wet hair and scared faces,
The coroner hauling truckloads of the dripping dead
To the Second Regiment armory where doctors waited
With useless pulmotors and the eight hundred motionless stiff
Lay ready for their relatives to pick them out on the floor
And take them home and call up an undertaker . . .

Well I was saying
My guts ain't ticklish about it.

I got imagination: I see a pile of three thousand dead people
Killed by the con[1], tuberculosis, too much work
        and not enough fresh air and green groceries

A lot of cheap roughnecks and the women and children of
    wops, and hardly any bankers and corporation lawyers or
    their kids, die from the con—three thousand a year in
    Chicago and a hundred and fifty thousand a year in the
    United States—all from the con and not enough fresh air
    and green groceries . . .

If you want to see excitement, more noise and crying than you
    ever heard in one of these big disasters the newsboys clean
    up on,
Go and stack in a high pile all the babies that die in Christian
    Philadelphia, New York, Boston and Chicago in one year
    because aforesaid babies haven't had enough good milk;
On top the pile put all the little early babies pulled from
    mothers willing to be torn with abortions rather than bring
    more children into the world—
Jesus! that would make a front page picture for the Sunday
    papers

---

[1] Consumption.

And you could write under it:
Morning glories
Born from the soil of love,
Yet now perished.

Have you ever stood and watched the kids going to work of a
  morning? White faces, skinny legs and arms, slouching along
  rubbing the sleep out of their eyes on the go to hold their
  jobs?

Can you imagine a procession of all the whores of a big town,
  marching and marching with painted faces and mocking
  struts, all the women who sleep in faded hotels and furnished
  rooms with any man coming along with a dollar or five
  dollars?

Or all the structural iron workers, railroad men and factory
  hands in mass formation with stubs of arms and stumps of
  legs, bodies broken and hacked while bosses yelled, "Speed—
  no slack—
  go to it!"?

Or two by two all the girls and women who go to the hind
  doors of restaurants and through the alleys and on the
  market street digging into the garbage barrels to get scraps
  of stuff to eat?

By the living Christ, these would make disaster pictures to paste
   on the front pages of the newspapers.

Yes, the *Eastland* was a dirty bloody job—bah!
              I see a dozen *Eastland*s
              Every morning on my way to work
              And a dozen more going home at night.

ANTI-WAR POEMS

PLANKED WHITEFISH

("I'm a going to live anyhow until I die."
—MODERN RAGTIME SONG)

Over an order of planked whitefish at a downtown club,
Horace Wild, the demon driver who hurled the first aeroplane
  that ever crossed the air over Chicago,
Told Charley Cutler, the famous rassler who never touches
  booze,
And Carl Sandburg, the distinguished poet now out of jail,
He saw near Ypres a Canadian soldier fastened on a barn door
  with bayonets pinning the hands and feet
And the arms and ankles arranged like Jesus at Golgotha 2,000
  years before
Only in northern France he saw
The genital organ of the victim amputated and placed between
  the lips of the dead man's mouth,
And Horace Wild, eating whitefish, looked us straight in the
  eyes,
And piled up circumstantial detail of what he saw one night
  running a truck pulling ambulances out of the mud near
  Ypres in November, 1915:
A box car next to a field hospital operating room . . . filled
  with sawed-off arms and legs . . .
Faces in the gray and the dark on the mud flats, white faces
  gibbering and loose convulsive arms making useless gestures,

And Horace Wild, the demon driver who loves fighting and can whip his weight in wildcats,

Pointed at a blue button in the lapel of his coat, "P-e-a-c-e" spelled in white letters, and he blurted:

"I don't care who the hell calls me a pacifist. I don't care who the hell calls me yellow. I say war is the game of a lot of God-damned fools."

ASHES AND DREAMS

Silence,
Dry sobs of darkness
In the houses and fields,
O mothers of the world,
Watching.

Hour on hour
The trenches call
And the ditches want
And the shovels wait.

White faces up,
Eyes wide and blind,
Legs stiff and arms limp,
Pass them along
And pile them in
And tumble them over,
Ashes and dreams together.

(Mothers of the world,
Your waste of work.)

VAUDEVILLE: 1916

I watch vaudeville. Two Swiss women whose bodies are perfect
  throw their legs and shoulders among trapezes and flying
  rings, a cross-play of flesh tights (and what are the babies
  doing since Russian and Austrian soldiers killed all the cows
  in Galicia?)
I watch vaudeville. A clown acrobat with a red mouth slashed
  on a death-white face tickles us all with mock danger and
  mock pain; he does handsprings on top of three tables
  pyramided and he double-somersaults from a flimsy ladder
  (and how long will the Crown Prince batter Joffre at Verdun
  and how long will French and Prussians cut each other, faces
  and guts, in the trenches and tunnels—and how long will the
  toy carvers of one nation drive their bayonets into the necks
  of toy carvers of another nation?)
I watch vaudeville. O we all watch vaudeville. And the Swiss
  women might carry beautiful children in pockets of flesh, in
  lovely red tissues where children hide. And the French clown
  acrobat with a red mouth slashed on a death-white face,
  maybe he has a cousin at Verdun, a cousin with an ear off
  and two ribs gone.
I watch vaudeville. O we all watch vaudeville. And the Crown
  Prince and Joffre over their breakfasts ask how the weather
  looks for new troop movements.

IMAGES

PAINTED FISHES

Green fishes on a red-lacquered tray
Are worn bringing a sea of beer
From draught-faucets to oak tables.
Between bartenders and customers
They are losing their green fins.

THESE VALLEYS SEEM OLD

(Dedicated to Mrs. Florence Ayscough who lives near Shanghai and whose translations from inscriptions on Chinese paintings furnished the basis for these renditions into modern American speech.)

1

The first frost comes now and turns the river water still and
    clear.
The sky is without a moon. Many stars show.
It is in the valleys near us the watch dogs are barking.
Across the water student lamplights shine.
My forehead burns and then a cold shakes me.
The chills go through my bones. I can hardly stand it.
Thoughts go back and forth about years now gone.
Let us keep off the fishing boats as we go home.

2

In the short grass valleys I lived with hard luck.
I was lonesome and it was no use to talk about it.
Now my wife nags at me to help her with the bamboo shoots
    for winter eating.
My boy is sick; none of his vegetables grow well this year.
About all I will have to live on is mouldy rice.
And dirty wine bought with promises will be about all for
    drink.
More and more bills are left at my door by tax collectors.
I lean heavy and slow on a stick and go tired to the house of
    my neighbor hoping he will have a little money for me.

3

The water never stops running in the stream at the foot of the
    mountains.
Spring over, green life comes up and shows itself deep between
    the mountains.
On all sides, Force wakes up, young sheep bleat, birds chirp
    learning to fly.
This mulberry thick with leaves was planted by a hand now
    forgotten. Who knows the name of it?

4

The wind blusters; we push off in our boat; we are going to
    pick water chestnuts.
We lean on our sticks and watch the sun set behind the villages
    to the west.
Among the apricot trees we see a fisherman standing with bent
    shoulders; he looks old.
And by the famous Peach Blossom Fountain homes of men
    stand in a cluster.

NAPOLEON

The little boy blew bubbles
Floating the air to glisten and shine
With a rainbow joy and airiness silken:
    They floated and broke and were gone.

The man blew bubbles,
Made nations and kings and captains
And armies that marched and slaughtered
And laughed at the blood on their hands—
    But the armies and kings and captains
    Are broken and vanished and gone.

The Workingmen

In the dusk of the dawn they go
A hundred thousand feet sluffing the sidewalks
Setting a dull-rumbling hum up the streets of the city.

PORTRAITS

MAGICAL CONFUSION

There was a lady we all knew.
(She gave the word "lady" its common meaning.)
Once she was named by a corset factory girl
I heard talking on a streetcar—
"The ladiest lady of all."

The mystery of little bugs,
Creepers and eaters so small the police, the army,
The many arms of law and government,
Captured none of them,
These of the mystery of little bugs,
Came to this lady at Sarasota,
On the sunny beach in Florida,
They began writing the doom they came for.

"Died today of pneumonia"
The wires clicked it off
To all the newspapers of the nation.
Readers of the news
Sitting on kegs in saloons,
Sitting on a wagon seat driving mules,
Sitting at windows knitting sox and rocking babies,

Sitting each one with an invisible bundle of thoughts
Slung on a shoulder like a Slav emigrant's
Handkerchief of knickknacks
To be kept a tight hold of—
So they read how the little bugs
Came and took the lady
And they knew there would never again
Be more pages in the papers
With pictures of the lady alive,
Shaking hands with somebody,
Pouring tea for somebody,
Wearing the clothes that mark a somebody,
Being in her acts and sayings
All that goes to form a somebody.

   The lady—
And she was a lady first
And a woman afterward,
Threw a purple silk shimmer
Into the word "exclusive"
Causing it to have the magical confusion
Of crossed spotlights of rainbow color—
Secretaries, butlers, guards, cooks, scullions,
Modistes and massage craftswomen
Shut the doors and put up the bars
And kept away
All the forces of vulgarization,

All eaters and creepers
Who take without warning or permit—
They were not among the exclusive who won entry—
Until the little bugs came
And the wires clicked it off: "Died of pneumonia."

PEARL DIVER

They call her a Pearl Diver . . . and laugh . . .
Because jewels not often fall into soup or salad.
She washes dishes, arms to elbows in greasy water in a big
 kitchen.
Outside 400 people are eating, and singers in low gowns are
 dancing among the tables.
Laughter and music break through the transoms and murmur
 death-whispers among the battering pans of the big kitchen.
She listens in the crashing tin and iron and porcelain and tries
 to pick out the fiddle love of the world coming through the
 transoms.
They call her a Pearl Diver . . . and laugh . . .

JERRY

Six years I worked in a knitting mill at a machine
And then I married Jerry, the iceman, for a change.
He weighed 240 pounds, and could hold me,
Who weighed 105 pounds, outward easily with one hand.
He came home drunk and lay on me with the breath of stale
  beer
Blowing from him and jumbled talk that didn't mean anything.
I stood it two years and one hot night when I refused him
And he struck his bare fist against my nose so it bled,
I waited till he slept, took a revolver from a bureau drawer,
Placed the end of it to his head and pulled the trigger.
From the stone walls where I am incarcerated for the natural
  term
Of life, I proclaim I would do it again.

Taking on Suds Men Talk

Taking on suds men talk. One bottle of near-beer
apiece was all Tom and I had. And he told the life
of a woman, his latest hotel find, as she told it to
him. Put short, as no life can be altogether told,
it was like this:

I married a well-off butcher. I didn't love him nor
hate him when I married him and it's the same now as
then. I married him because he went to bed and said
he would never eat again unless I married him. He
starved two days. His mother cried to my mother and
to me. So we went and got a license.

Until he died two years ago, the family doctor used
me when he wanted me. He sent letters saying my health
must not run down. I showed these letters to my husband
and then went to the doctor's office.

A dentist who used me I could never understand. He drilled
one tooth five months and loved me like wild every
time I sat in the big chair and he straightened my knees
and feet on the extensions. Though he went as far as love
could go with me, he always sent bills for services.

Once I was sick three months. I told my mother how I was.
She said it was a baby. I told her it would be terrible to
have a doctor run a knife across my belly. Then my
mother told me there is no knife when a baby is born. She said
"It comes out the same place it goes in." Why did no one
tell me this till so late?

The baby came. It was a beautiful baby and strong. Why did
it live only two years? I don't know what it died of. Some-
times I think it was afraid of our house, something wrong,
and didn't want to grow up with us.

I found out my husband was trying to get a sixteen year
old girl neighbor. He was telling me, "If you go with other
men I kill you." I made a date with the family doctor that
week and kept it.

We have money from the butcher shop. I took piano lessons. I
know elocution and recite long poems. And all the time I am
hunting more life—nothing satisfies me—what will become of
me?

African Americans

Elizabeth Umpstead

I am Elizabeth Umpstead, dead at seventy-five years of age, and they are taking me in a polished and silver-plated box today, and an undertaker, assured of cash for his work, will supply straps to let the box down the lean dirt walls, while a quartet of singers—assured of cash for their work, sing "Nearer My God to Thee," and a clergyman, also assured of cash for his services—will pronounce the words: "Dust to dust and ashes to ashes."

I am gone from among the two-legged moving figures on top the earth now, and nobody will say my heart is someway wrong when I assert, I was the most beautiful nigger girl in northern Indiana; and men wanted my beauty, white men and black men—they wanted to take it and crush it and taste it—and I learned what they wanted and I traded on it; I schemed and haggled to get all I could for it—and so, I am one nigger girl who today has a grand funeral with all the servitors paid in spot cash.

I learned early, away back in short dresses, when a lawyer took me and used me the same as a brass cuspidor or a new horse and buggy or a swivel chair or anything that gives more life-ease for spot cash—he paid $600 cash to me for the keep of the child of my womb and his loins. And then he went to a revival, sang "Jesus Knows All about Our Troubles," moaned he was a sinner and wanted Jesus to wash his sins away. He joined the church and stood up one night before hundreds of people and blabbed to them

45

how he used me, had a child by me, and paid me $600 cash. And I waited till one night I saw him in the public square and I slashed his face with a leather horsewhip, calling all the wild crazy names that came to my tongue to damn him and damn him and damn him, for a sneak in the face of God and man.

BLACK PROPHETESS

I makes my livin' washin'.
I keeps happy at the feet of Jesus.
My husband ain't saved; he's wicked:
but the Bible says a sanctified wife
shall sanctify her husband and save him.

I'm livin' in Chicago
but I calls Ohio my home
because I lived in Cincinnati
an' Columbus an' Toledo
an' I was in Dayton
a week before the waters swept Dayton
an' I stood on the public square
an' warned 'em of destruction.

I got four permits from the police in Chicago
to stand on the street corners
and warn the people of destruction.
I told 'em about the *Eastland* and the war
before those things happened.

Three years ago the police gave me my last permit
to warn the people of destruction

an' I got a right to stand on any corner
south of Twelfth Street.

They tell me it's a free country
an' I can talk God's destruction all I want
just so I don't come downtown.

I got five daughters.
The oldest is in Philadelphia.
She makes prophecies too.

I make prophecies when the spirit moves me.
Yesterday I felt the spirit stirrin' me up.
I saw blood up to the bridles of the horses.
I saw the mark of the Beast.
(When the Bible speaks of a Beast it means a King.)
The Kings all got to go.

God is cleansing the earth.
He's goin' to make it all clean
and Jesus is goin' to come again
an' live a thousand years.

I go to the newspapers with my prophecies
but they don't print 'em.

If you print this—
when will it be in the paper?

CLEO

Born of a slave mother and father, she toiled
in the fields, loved the earth and the sun,
and was strong.

At evening the going down of the sun told her
whether she was written in the book of God as
a good or a bad woman for that day.

In the gloaming of a long autumn day she told
friends, "Every one of us got a baby inside de
body. When de rest of de body shuffle off, dis
baby go to Jesus. Dare is wings waitin' to be
hitched on. Atter dat, you is angel."

The fields and the earth were kind to her.

MAN, THE MAN-HUNTER

I saw Man, the man-hunter,
Hunting with a torch in one hand
And a kerosene can in the other,
Hunting with guns, ropes, shackles.

    I listened
    And the high cry rang.
The high cry of Man, the man-hunter:
We'll get you yet,   you   Son of a Bitch!

    I listened later,
    The high cry rang:
Kill him! kill him!   the Judean equivalent   the Son of a Bitch!

In the morning the sun saw
Two butts of something, a smoking rump,
And a warning in charred wood:
                Well, we got him,
              the   Son of a Bitch.

A
Reporter's
Poems

DAILIES

I am on the streets all the time,
  day and night.
I am rushed to the hands of the people,
  The mob, demos.
High power motorcars take me with speed
  to the hands of the millions.
I am out in the rain and sun where men work:
  I am the daily newspaper.

Books? They stand clean and dreaming
             on shelves in houses.
I am dirty and always fighting.
        The people want me.

MONDAY, ONE P.M.

Fix it up like an affidavit with a notary's seal: Sworn to before
   me this day—'twon't do any good in this case—either you
   get it or you don't.

I dropped into the I.W.W. headquarters and talked with Bill
   Haywood and Russ, Italian and Slovak organizers handling
   a strike at Pullman
And Haywood was wondering how in hell Robert T. Lincoln,
   chairman of the board of directors of the Pullman Company,
   ever sprang from the loins of Abraham Lincoln, the finest
   guy of all of 'em in American history
And the Russ organizer said the Pullman officers were a lot
   of liars telling the newspapers a ten per cent pay raise was
   going to all the Pullman workers
And the Slovak swore and said women were going crazy out
   at Pullman trying to raise families and keep their boys and
   girls straight on nineteen cents an hour for yard-men and
   roustabouts.

Well, I picked up a telephone to call Amy Lowell at the
   Congress Hotel and tell her what a good job she did writing
   about the life of Emile Verhaeren, the Belgian working-class
   poet.

It was a party line and two men were talking. One said: May
  Blossom is the greatest bitch in the world; she's only six
  months old but you can count on it she's the greatest bitch
  the world has ever seen.
How does she behave?—came the query; and the answer was:
  You never saw a bulldog bitch in your life more gentle;
  I raised her myself; I would trust my mother with her.
And the talk ran on litters and whelps, brindles and fawns,
  ending with the price of May Blossom, rated as the world's
  greatest bitch, fixed at one hundred seventy-five dollars.

And when they hung up I got Amy at the Congress. I told her I
  was sorry I missed her lecture on Imagism the night before at
  the Little Theatre and I'd like to come over and ask her some
  questions about Emile Verhaeren, the Belgian working-class
  poet.
Amy said she just finished breakfast one o'clock in the
  afternoon, she reads all night instead of sleeping, and she'd
  try to arrange her program so I'd get a look-in.
I told her I felt kind of restless about the new poetry and I had
  high hopes the new poetry one way or another would be
  able to get at the real stuff of American life, slipping its
  fingers into the steel meshes and copper coils of it under the
  streets and over the houses and people and factories and
  groceries, conceding a fair batting average to Dante and
  Keats for what they wrote about love and roses and the
  moon.

Big Stones of the Egyptian Tombs

I was a tomb of the Pharaohs.
I stood in Egypt 4,000 years.
Then I was hauled by camels to a Suez port.
A long steel steamboat carried me to New York
And a railroad train fetched me to Chicago.
Horses tugging in leather harness
Brought me to the Field Museum of Natural History,
Where I had a short rest of twenty-eight years.
But today they loaded me onto a motor truck
And I heard the cylinders and transmission
Go chug-chug, chiz-chiz—noises like we never had
In Egypt.
I wonder if the mummies of the Pharaohs
Shivered when the driver whistled at magistrates
In blue coats and brass buttons on the street corners.
I never heard so many new noises.
I think the Pharaohs who are now sleeping
Along in their fortieth centuries of sleep
Would say this racket is scandalous.
I am comforted, however.
The new building where they are putting me up
For citizens, travelers, school children to look at,

The new building is nearer the heart of the city,
And if I don't like the hot dusty heart of the city
There is always the blue peace of the big blue Lake Michigan.

THE REWRITE MAN IS TIRED

The body of a woman found dead in a trunk
opened in a railroad express warehouse
is the focal point of a fresh mystery
succeeding other mysteries. Who she was,
who killed her and why—if we knew this
how much would we know?

The high school psychology teacher who shot
the wife of a horse doctor who was her para-
mour, the mystery there is how she occupies her
time in the Wisconsin penitentiary and who the
horse doctor spends his leisure time with now.

The returned overseas lieutenant who shot his
enceinte wife, and a hobo he had paid to execute
a fake highway robbery, was planning to take $1,500
of his wife's money, all she had, and another woman
off somewhere to romance and new life—the mystery
is whether he could look a man-eating gorilla in
the face and say, "Brother."

The ethical culture woman of the higher life,
spiritual bride of the victrola salesman who was 52

against her 36, shot herself and died after wrecking
his optic nerve and sending him blind for life—the
mystery is how she could do it after reading Emerson.

The rich oil promoter found dead in a hotel next room
to his paramour lady killed himself, all experts agree,
and his wife was an ideal mother and steadfast spouse,
the experts also agree—the mystery is what he and the
affinity quarrelled about before he gave himself the
fatal lead pill.

The Kentucky girl with black eyes did a job that has
less mystery than any—they found her and the advertising
man in bed together sunken deep in the weights of farewell
six-shooter messages—they were both tired and have gone
to a good rest—and the diary of the black-eyed Kentucky
girl sings a wonderful bittersweet love—life and death
were a long mix of bittersweet for the two of them—his
family is well taken care of, she had no family—and any
poet writing of them will wish the ghosts to walk softly
over their graves.

Otherwise one might say politely or otherwise—Goddam
these triangles—they don't get what they pay
for—the silver moons of winter and the blood moons of
autumn call them quitters squinting at life's chiaroscuro.

A Reporter in Debt

The poet who kept himself in debt
knowing the big stream of people
live with their feet and shoulders
clambering through pits of debt,
the poet spoke easy:
"why should I be free who must write chains?
how shall I write chains unless the steel
clutches my wrists and ankles?
unless I am dirty and dusty from the pits
how can I write the people of the pits?"

EDGAR LEE MASTERS

To Webster Ford

A man wrote two books.

One held in its covers the outside man whose name was on a
Knox College diploma, who bought his clothes at Marshall
Field's, had his name done by a sign painter in gilt on an
office door in a Loop skyscraper, and never did any damage
to the code of morals set forth by the Chicago *Tribune*.

The other book held a naked man, the sheer brute under the
clothes as he will be stripped at the Last Day, the inside man
with red heartbeats that go on always ticking off life against
the ribs.

Scratched into portraits, here are the villagers, all those who
walked on Main Street, the folks he knew down on Illinois
prairies where his grandmother raised eleven boys and life
was a repetitive epic of corn and hogs.

The shadow of his soul touched the shadows of their souls as
he loved them and his fingers knew something about the fine
dust of their blood after they are dead and the silence of love
and the strangeness of dreams that haunt their graves.

SHADOWS OF APRIL AND BLUE HILLS

Shadows of April and blue hills, smoke of purple gardens and
roaming wisteria, around Lee Masters' head sometimes. In a
mixing harvest haze of things born and growing . . . legs in a
climb of twisted mountain roads to a music of red laughter,
red mouths. Faces of women and baby hands, baby hands
all by themselves . . . and the beautiful violet eyes of John P.
Altgeld in the coffin where he lay for his last public parade.
I say—this all swims around Lee's head some days for the
dreamers who know him.

And some days the shadows lose all blue of April hills and red
mountain laughter. The shadows then are piles of culm at
a coal pit—shapeless grotesques blotting the horizon. No
faces . . . it is the same as air halfway between here and
Canopus . . . it is the slate gray of Schopenhauer. Lee pounds
with a tack hammer on a tall, steel door opening into other
tall, steel doors leading to further successions of tall, steel doors.

EDGAR LEE MASTERS

They came to my office as clients
And told me their secrets,
Where they had gotten money
Or how their women were faithless
Or their daughters and sons became liars.
I made them into a book
And the *Manchester Guardian*
Credits me with tremendous imagination.

I should have put myself in the book.
A head full of suspicions
Breeding prolific as rats in a garret
Where winter corn is stored.
How shall a man be a reputable lawyer
And not turn to a creature of suspicions?
I am suspicious of the moon
Being something else than the astronomers proclaim.
I must write of the moon and how it is like
The people in *The Spoon River Anthology*,
Either a hypocrite eaten with dark secrets,
Or a woman with sex unsatisfied,
Or a man with a phallus for a god,

69

Or a thief or a pimp
Or a shivering puppet of fate.
As a lawyer I know the moon must be a fake
Like all the rest of us.

It is not easy to be a great man.
There are always thieves lurking about
Trying to steal the sunlight
Shining through your halo.
All great men are lonely
Because their greatness is a load
And fills their veins with the spirochete
And sometimes they feel like vomiting
On the whole human race
Because it does not properly acknowledge
Their greatness.

It is hell to be a great man
As it is also hell to be almost great,
Not quite great enough for greatness,
Alone among the brass cuspidors of a lawyer's office.

On Re-reading Edgar Lee Masters' Lincoln-the-Man Three Years after the First Reading

Have it your way and make yourself satisfied.
Rest back in the satisfaction of what you make of it.
The man Lincoln was everything you say he was.
Of this you are sure with a lawyer's certainty.
You have examined the evidence and fathomed it.
And now you pronounce your final judgements.
In a tone of finality you say what you say.
And of course none of the animals is in it.
You are risen above the ways of the animals.
The fang of the dripping hot blood
This was Lincoln's but is not yours.
The eyes of lust hunting for the kill
And licking it, lapping it, when at last
It lay writhing in wounds red for the drinking
This too was Lincoln's but is not yours.
A painted ship on a painted ocean is only paint.
Your pinnacle for seeing, your high point for considering
Stands far and aloft as a reality
With a holy light and a dedicated zeal—yes? and what have you?

One or two of your allegations of fact
Five or six particulars offered as beyond dispute
Tricks of the trade of the hack orator
Devices of the smalltime shyster
Maulings of an iconoclast with a wooden hammer
An idolater idolizing his lack of idols
A finder finding he has found a great nothing
And therefore he must sing of this nothing
And of how nothing plus nothing equals who? what? where?
And looky-here looky-there and now-see-what
Because goddam-it the halo is a lot of hooey
And jesus-wept the big toe is tarnished
And all the myrrh and frankincense just a pile of shit.
Sure the decisions were either hangovers of the St. Louis blues
Or spitballs of malice and spite
Of the bewilderment of a commander never meant for
    command
Sure and the letters and speeches
The many various attempts at argument and persuasion
They were motivated by the bible of the Jews and their
    Jehovah
Along with the intricate malicious wishes
Of the goddamdest lowdown puritans ever on record
For hypocrisy is living and deceit is dying.
Yessir we know well in your slovenly meandering book
You are making for us a true portrait of Abe Lincoln.
Sure. Of course it ain't a portrait of yourself.

No you didn't get into the book.
You were the consummate artist that kept yourself hid.
Yes. And is that so? And maybe you are in the book.
And possibly the book is a mirroring of Lee Masters.
Maybe you stand out bigger from the book than Lincoln.
Perhaps you have written yourself down for what you are.

This has been done. There are cases.
What you say counts along with the way you say it.
The way you say it may tell more than what you are saying.
You can't do a package like this without fingerprints.
Your autograph is there on every page
Trying to scrawl itself in letters insistent
On shining in contrast
With the oft repeated scribble
Of the incessantly signed name: A. Lincoln.
Behold we have here now a something
And if you will listen to me and watch me a moment or two
You will see that the something changes into nothing.
Where was a delusive fragrance now exists a stench.
This supposed aroma of health is one ordinary stink.
Smell with me as we proceed in the analysis
Of the interrelated action of the atoms and protons
And you will see how what was considered
A mystic substance endowed with the majesty of the sea
Is after all the evidence is in

Just one more pathetic slob lost in his own slobber
A peasant crafty with pretenses of manner
Yet a lackadaisical snot-nose to the very finish
The indubitable testimonies standing forth that
He did not know which hand to wipe his ass with.

 Yes Lee Masters you have proved your case.
And you kept yourself out of the book and gave us Lincoln.
And your own devices of rhetoric never get in your way.
And you are no victim of any propagandas whatsoever.
And your humility grows by what it feeds on.
And new civilizations shall thrive on your offerings.
And you have dedicated yourself anew to several proposi-
 tions.
In this case you have not proven yourself a shyster—no.
The liar forgets, the liar's memory fails—but not yours.
Your interpretation is final
And no one is so sure of its finality as you yourself.
Your verdict is comprised in a few words.
 "Lincoln was a rat and a snake."
Or: "Lincoln lived, writhed, killed, and was himself killed.
 Better it would have been that he should not be killed
 when he was yet better that he should never have been
 born."
 With this you Lee Masters get by.
 You have fathomed the evidence
 And written down Lincoln or Lee Masters
 One of the two.

Rest back and sit satisfied.
The halo is a lot of hooey,
Lincoln and Masters one more fable,
One more conglomerate fart
Lost on the anxious rumps of the west wind.

LOVE POEMS

In Blue Gown and
in Black Satin Gown

she wore a blue gown for him once
the fabric flowing with her curves
only the hair of long black eyelashes
flashing naked for his eyes:
a mist of wanting gathered
a black-ice loneliness between them:
    she loosened the blue gown
    and lay bare before him
        a smooth miracle of dawn
        a silent shingle of lights—
            so they hid themselves
            in a winding sheet of passion
            in a little hut of shaken walls

she wore a black satin gown for him once
the flow of her hips a poem of night
moving in a dusk of her long eyelashes
    standing they held a greeting kiss
    murmured of the ritual to come
        she lay waiting for him
        lifting the black satin

gleaming over a white navel
she drew him in with familiar sheaths
they lay in a room of blood-rose shadows
hearing many clocks in a music of bronze
in flesh tones of a cool vesper twilight
slowly they moved into storm and drums
into a whirl of changing light-spokes
her white torso lost in satin shadows
sank in a moan of white blossoms
in a falling sheen of black moonlight.

The First Kiss Came with Flame

the first kiss came with flame
she gave him a flame wine
from her scarlet lips a flame wine

the second kiss came with a sea-wish
she became the sea to him
the pride and anger of the sea she gave him

three times they had kissed
a third time deep in her winding sea-velvet
she moved in light-shafts of bright sea-velvet for him

again she came with a long kiss of stars
she beckoned him to a tall dome of stars

SHE HELD HERSELF
A DEEP POOL FOR HIM

she held herself a deep pool for him
and the shadows crying for him
he gathered himself in many dark waters
and the shadows crying for her
they took each other in shadow meetings
they held themselves in shadow songs

    she coiled herself around him
    with a ribbon of glass
    and a rope of gold
    the coils of her cunning held him
    with rings of golden glass
    with a moon of melting gold
    with a mist of sunset ribbons

AN INTERWOVEN MAN
AND WOMAN TALKED

An interwoven man and woman talked.
The mesh of a red rose held the man.
A moist evening dew beheld the two.
Their speech was in even vocabularies.
Their voices comprised several violins.
The lights of changing weather were there.
They talked of kingdoms, empires, republics.
They spoke of mice, dice, republicans, democrats,
How stars may be foiled of grand desires,
How love may be wept over as an abstraction,
How black velvet may suddenly transfuse
With tracks and spatters of red blood,
How fate waits at a door with a white finger,
How beautiful children become drab vagabonds,
How the coin of life comes willy-nilly,
How Jesus was not ashamed of miracles.

HELLCAT

He had arguments about a woman.
He argued to himself about her.
She was a hellcat, he argued.
Crazy, never the same two minutes.
Yet her breasts were hills of passion,
Her tongue made for swift kissing,
Her torso holding sanctuaries
Strange as the lost temples
Of sunken archipelagoes—
She carried sacraments for him
Yet his words for her were hellcat,
Crazy woman.

TROTH TRYST

There is a troth between us.
A troth means we are to keep
a tryst.
A tryst means we shall drop into
a dappled sea together.
The sea is a grand smooth clamor,
bitter with fish, drowsy with dream
blossoms.

LITERARY

AND HISTORICAL

FIGURES

ARMS

(For Wallace Stevens)

Renoir goes on painting.
A man from south France tells me it is so.
One picture a day, good or bad, the old man goes on.
And a little work every day on one big picture for God
    and children and remembered women.
So Renoir, his right arm no good anymore
And the left arm half gone,
So Renoir goes on.

And when you come again
We will go to the Edelweiss for jazz
Or to Hester's dirty place on the river
Or to some Chinese dump where they bring what you want
    and no questions asked,
And I will ask you why Renoir does it
And I believe you will tell me.

DUNSANY

Dunsany, soldier, vagabond, horseman, dreamer,
Was exploited by the lah-de-dah intelligentsia.
Fat-assed and fog-headed women who never read
His books got a conception of him as a real gent
Who could tickle their gizzards with courtesy,
Suavity, severity of demeanour, and all the props
Of a titled lord. He came, he pissed against the
Legs of the grand pianos, he spit on the rugs and walls,
Everywhere except in the cuspidors, and the more
They lah-de-dahed about art and the drayma the
More he yawned and tied new knots with his long
Folded arms and fixed new designs and arrangements
Of his long legs and wished to God he was on a
Saddle pony loping through mist on a sea road
Anywheres in the British isles.

VIRGINIA WOOLF

Virginia Woolf left her home in England, near the sea,
    and went for a walk.
Her steps led her to the bank of a tidal river.
She walked out into the sea till she became a part of the river
    and the sea.

She was tired of the land.
And being tired of time, too, she turned her back on it
    and walked into a timeless beyond named eternity.

For the nice strange, incalculable quality of her mind
    we may go to her books.
You don't know where you go from here.
The nonsense and thin airy fantasy at times is not ridiculous
    but sublime.
The British Empire—her special and personal British Empire—
    floats and sways as a bundle of toy balloons.
"This ivory dome of mine," Virginia Woolf seemed often to
    imply, "has pavilions and people that forget they belong to
    the regular and established order—they don't belong!"

In this hour of the world with the smoke and stench over most
   of it what a book she could have written about why she
   wanted to belong to the sea, forever, to be no more on the
   land.
She was tall, gaunt, long-necked, having a touch in head and
   face of Rosetti's "The Blessed Damozel."
Why she walked into tidal waters of the sea for a fadeout
   no one can tell.
Reverence for her mind and heart goes on.
She represented things money cannot buy nor children be
   taught.

HAWTHORNE

Nathaniel Hawthorne lived under an arch of glooms.
Invisible scarves of undertaker's crepe
Twisted at his throat to fasten on him
And he fought forever lifelong
The winds whipping to fasten these scarves.

Between two ears under a bone dome: caverns,
Or if we so choose: dank tarns:
And here he swam forever lifelong
Round and round in the destiny of a brass bowl
Lined with an inner dark of sea-green tarnish.

The wind whipping those scarves, of course,
Is another metaphor.

MOTHER ALPHONSA

Mother Alphonse was named Rose
when she was born, the daughter
of Nathaniel and Sophia Hawthorne.

Her father had dark eyes and sad thoughts.
He died, during a great war, and a fine friend
said, "He became too lonely to live."

The daughter too was a writer with a gleaming pen.
The world overcame her with its many desolations.
She founded a sisterhood called Servants of Relief
    for Incurable Cancer.
At Rosary Hill Home and at St. Rose's the doors were
    opened to victims "without friends and utterly
    without resources."

She could have gone on and written many books
and she would have been welcomed at tea parties
and at gatherings on lawns of evenings.
Yet she chose to work with the completely forsaken.

DANIEL WEBSTER

What is more baffling to men than glory
and what does a leader mean after an exploit
telling his men, "There is glory enough for all"?
Why should Daniel Webster walk with a friend
in the white moonlight coming on the Capitol
and shining in the black patches of oak and chestnut
saying, "I have done absolutely nothing—
At thirty Alexander had conquered the world—
and I am forty."
Then came his orations in the United States Senate
when the country, the world, listened, and the name
came to him of the world's greatest orator.
When at last he lay dying he believed a deathbed
oration was wanted from him; he had lived an orator
and would die in the oracular manner.
He made sure the family was assembled; he saw a scribe
settled with pen and ink and paper to take the final
locutions on life, death, the afterlife, and a "crepuscular"
halfworld known to the ancients.
The body of him was a languishing instrument yet the brain
still held that adjective "crepuscular" and the dying tongue
could announce the syllables "cre-pus-cu-lar."

Trying to fathom and gather immortality as an idea weakened him and he sank on the pillow, closed his eyes, and almost passed out to the other realm.

Then he rallied, opened his eyes, pivoted once more with his leonine head, and asked, "Have I—wife, son, doctor, friends, are you all here?—have I, on this occasion, said anything unworthy of Daniel Webster?"

Seldom do orators die in so oratorical a manner.

Eugene V. Debs

On his face as he lay, at peace at last, in Terre Haute,
There was the majestic trajectory of a trail from the earth
to the stars.
The cotillions of the Milky Way could not bewilder him
by their numbers.
He had always dreamed of paths difficult for human feet,
bridges impossible to the calculations of accepted
engineers, union depots open to all the races and languages
of man.
He was a railroad man, familiar to the link and coupling
pin, to rain, zero weather, snow plows, stalled engines, the
first Brotherhood of Railroad Firemen, the first American
Railway Union.
He was an orator, a jailbird, a presidential candidate, an
enemy of war, a convict, a philosopher, storyteller, friend
of man.
Said a poet, "He had ten hopes to your one."

A sister laid a spray of four Crusader red roses
on his breast.

Over in Valhalla, if Valhalla is not demolished, rebuilt,
renamed, he speaks at ease with Garrison, John Brown,
Albert Parsons, Spartacus.

SHERWOOD ANDERSON

To write one book in five years
or five books in one year,
to be the painter and the thing painted,
the writer and the written of
—where are we, bo?

Wait. Get the number of this guy.

The barbershop handling is not all
nor the tweeds, the cheviot, the Scotch mist,
nor the flame orange scarf.

On looks he is "bushwah"[1]—

And yet—he sleeps under bridges with lonely
crazy men; he sits in country jails with icono-
clasts and sab cats[2]; he drinks beer with broken-

---

[1] bourgeois.
[2] sab cat—a logger's name for an expert at sabotage; named for the black cat pictured on an I.W.W. emblem.

down burlesque actresses; he has cried with a
heart full of tears for Windy MacPherson's father;
he draws pencil sketches of the wrists of lonely
women whose flowers are ashes.

Can a man sit at a desk in a skyscraper in Chicago, Illinois,
and be a harnessmaker in a corn town in Iowa
and feel the tall grass coming up in June
and the ache of the cottonwood trees
singing with the prairie wind?

Ask this guy. Get his number.

EZRA [Pound]

Good reading good reading
O most excellent reading
If can easy pass over
Easy skip idiotics
    pedantics pomposities
Good reading sure sure
I have learnt
    how to read Ez
He is my crazy brudder

Sacco

and

Vanzetti

LEGAL MIDNIGHT HOUR

Well, the dying time came, the legal midnight hour,
The moment set by law for the Chair to be at work,
To substantiate the majesty of the State of Massachusetts
That hour was at hand, had arrived, was struck by the clocks,
The time for two men to be carried cool on a cooling board
Beyond the immeasurably thin walls between day and night,
Beyond the reach of airmail, telegrams, radiophones,
Beyond the brotherhoods of blood into the fraternities
Of mist and foggy dew, of stars and ice.
　　The time was on for two men
　　To march beyond blood into dust—
　　A time that comes to all men,
　　Some with a few loved ones at a bedside,
　　Some alone in the wilderness or the wide sea,
　　Some before a vast audience of all mankind.

　　Now Sacco saw the witnesses
　　As the straps were fitted on
　　Tying him down in the Chair—
　　And seeing the witnesses were
Respectable men and responsible citizens
And even though there had been no introductions,

Sacco said, "Good-evening, gentlemen."
And before the last of the straps was fastened so to hold
Sacco murmured, "Farewell, mother."

Then came Vanzetti.
He wished the vast audience of all mankind
To know something he carried in his breast.
This was the time to tell it.
He had to speak now or hold his peace forever.
The headgear was being clamped on.
The straps muffling his mouth were going on.
He shouted, "I wish to forgive some people
        for what they are now doing."
    And so now
    the dead are dead? ? ? ?

Daydream

of a Radical

Poet

I Should Like to Be Hanged
on a Summer Afternoon

I have often thought I should like to be hanged
On a summer afternoon in daylight, the sun shining and bands
    playing,
In a park or on a public square or a main street corner,
    everybody in town looking on and talking about it,
Newspaper extras spelling my name in tall headlines telling the
    town I am getting hanged.

And I smile to the sheriff and say he will be laughed at if the
    rope breaks
And he goes puttering, solemn, doing a duty under the law,
Feeling the ropes, searching corners, testing scantlings.

And before the cap is drawn over my head
And before my feet are tied for the straight drop,
When I am asked if I have any last word to say before I go to
    meet my God and Maker;
I speak in a cool, even voice, fixing my eyes maybe on some
    dark-eyed mother in the crowd, a grown dark-eyed daughter
    leaning against her.

I speak and say, "I am innocent and I am ready to meet my
God face to face" . . .

I have often thought I should like to be hanged that way on a
summer afternoon in daylight, the sun shining and bands
playing.

NOTES

"Billy Sunday" appeared in the September 1915 issues of *The Masses* and the *International Socialist Review*.

"God's Children" is previously unpublished.

"The *Eastland*" is previously unpublished. A few lines were quoted in Penelope Niven's *Carl Sandburg: A Biography* (New York: Charles Scribner's Sons, 1991), 264.

"Planked Whitefish" is previously unpublished.

"Ashes and Dreams" appeared in the May 1915 issue of the *International Socialist Review*. It is also quoted in Niven's *Carl Sandburg*, 259.

"Vaudeville: 1916" is previously unpublished.

"Painted Fishes" is previously unpublished.

"These Valleys Seem Old" is previously unpublished.

"Napoleon" is previously unpublished.

"The Workingmen" is previously unpublished.

"Magical Confusion" is previously unpublished.

"Pearl Diver" is previously unpublished.

"Jerry" is previously unpublished.

"Taking on Suds Men Talk" is previously unpublished.

"Elizabeth Umpstead" appeared in Norman Corwin's *The World of Carl Sandburg* (New York: Harcourt Brace & World, 1961) but was never collected.

"Black Prophetess" is previously unpublished.

"Cleo" is previously unpublished.

The revised version of "Man, the Man-Hunter" is included in *The Complete Poems of Carl Sandburg* (New York: Harcourt Brace Jovanovich, 1970).

"Dailies" is previously unpublished.

"Monday, One P.M." is previously unpublished.

"Big Stones of the Egyptian Tombs" appeared in the Chicago *Daily News*, undated clipping. Title provided by the editors.

"The Rewrite Man Is Tired" is previously unpublished.

"The Reporter in Debt" is part of a letter to Louis Untermeyer, September 26, 1919. Title provided by the editors.

"To Webster Ford" appeared in the November 1914 issue of *Reedy's Mirror*. It was never collected.

"Shadows of April and Blue Hills" is previously unpublished. Title provided by the editors.

"Edgar Lee Masters" is previously unpublished.

"On Re-Reading Edgar Lee Masters' Lincoln-the-Man Three Years after the First Reading" is previously unpublished.

"In Blue Gown and in Black Satin Gown" is previously unpublished. Title provided by the editors.

"The First Kiss Came with Flame" is previously unpublished. Title provided by the editors.

"She Held Herself a Deep Pool for Him" is previously unpublished. Title provided by the editors.

"An Interwoven Man and Woman Talking" is previously unpublished. Title provided by the editors.

"Hellcat" is previously unpublished. Title provided by the editors.

"Troth Tryst" is previously unpublished.

"Arms" is previously unpublished.

"Dunsany" is on a printed card in the Sandburg Archives in the University of Illinois at Urbana-Champaign Library. It was never collected.

"Virginia Woolf" is previously unpublished. Title provided by the editors.

"Hawthorne" is previously unpublished. Title provided by the editors.

"Mother Alphonsa" is previously unpublished.

"Daniel Webster" is previously unpublished.

"Eugene V. Debs" is previously unpublished.

"Sherwood Anderson" was published in expurgated form under the title "Portrait" in *Smoke and Steel*.

"Ezra" appears in Niven's *Carl Sandburg*, 584. It was never collected.

"Legal Midnight Hour" is previously unpublished.

"I Should Like to Be Hanged on a Summer Afternoon" is previously unpublished. Title provided by the editors.

The only dated poem in this collection is "The Reporter in Debt." Most of these selections, however, appear to have been written before 1930.

ACKNOWLEDGMENTS AND CREDITS

We are indebted to the Sandburg Family Trust (Maurice C. Green-baum and Frank M. Parker, trustees) and to the University Library at the University of Illinois at Urbana-Champaign for permission to edit and publish these poems. For a long period of time we have received help and encouragement with our Sandburg studies from Maurice C. Greenbaum; Frank M. Parker; Margaret, Janet, and Helga Sandburg; Penelope Niven; Carl Deal; Sarah and Eric Jourdain; and John Hoffmann. We are grateful for their assistance.

We are also deeply indebted to Vicki Austin, our editor at Harcourt Brace & Company, for her guidance in seeing this work to completion.

There are twelve illustrations in this volume. We list them in order of appearance and with our titles for the purpose of identification:

Billy Sunday Preaching in 1915, by George Bellows, from *Metropolitan Magazine,* May 1915, p. 9.

Pulling Up the Drowned of the Eastland, *International Socialist Review,* September 1915, p. 135.

Wagon Load of the Dead, from Laurence Stallings, *The First World War* (New York: Simon and Schuster, 1933), p. 92.

Factory Workers, Culver Pictures.

Woman Seated on Steps, Doris Ulmann, c. 1930, platinum print, University of New Mexico Art Museum; purchase through the Julius L. Rolshoven Memorial Fund.

Prophetess, © Doris Ulmann, *The Darkness and the Light* (New York: Aperture, 1974), p. 15.

Sandburg the Reporter, courtesy the University Library at the University of Illinois at Urbana-Champaign.

Edgar Lee Masters in 1915, from Masters' *Across Spoon River* (New York: Farrar and Rinehart, 1936), frontispiece.

The Sandburgs in Their Garden, courtesy Helga Sandburg.

Eugene Debs and Helga Sandburg, courtesy Helga Sandburg.

Sacco and Vanzetti, courtesy the Trustees of the Boston Public Library.

The Young Sandburg, courtesy the University Library at the University of Illinois at Urbana-Champaign.

ABOUT THE EDITORS

George Hendrick is Professor of English at the University of Illinois at Urbana-Champaign. His publications include *Henry Salt: Humanitarian Reformer and Man of Letters; Remembrances of Concord and the Thoreaus; Toward the Making of Thoreau's Modern Reputation* (with Fritz Oehlschlaeger); *Thoreau Amongst Friends and Philistines, and Other Thoreauviana; Ever the Winds of Chance* (with Margaret Sandburg); *Fables, Foibles, and Foobles*; and *To Reach Eternity: The Letters of James Jones.*

Willene Hendrick is an independent scholar who lives in Urbana, Illinois. With George Hendrick she has published *On the Illinois Frontier: Dr. Hiram Rutherford, 1840–1848; Katherine Anne Porter*, revised edition; *The Savour of Salt: A Henry Salt Anthology*; and *Ham Jones, Antebellum Southern Humorist: An Anthology.*